101 THINGS EVERY BOY NEEDS TO KNOW

Important Life Advice for Teenage Boys!

Jamie Myers

ISBN: 978-1-957590-27-1

For questions, email: Support@AwesomeReads.org

Please consider writing a review!

Just visit: AwesomeReads.org/review

FREE BONUS

SCAN TO GET OUR NEXT BOOK FOR FREE!

TABLE OF CONTENTS

INTRODUCTION

Most men do not figure out who they are, what they believe in, and what they want out of their lives until they are adults. However, childhood is the most formative part of a man's life. Learning to understand yourself and your goals from boyhood can help you succeed in your youth and as an adult too. Unfortunately, most men learn this fact too late to apply it to their own lives.

That is why it is important to start learning about yourself, your life, and the world as soon as possible. The sooner you start learning, the better off you will be. You can make the most out of your youth and apply what you have learned to create an adult life that excites and fulfills you.

Whether you are a parent trying to raise your son to become a respectful, successful, and well-meaning adult or a boy yourself wanting to do everything in your power to be the best version of yourself, it can be difficult to find resources and tips that are applicable to your life now and in the future. Most articles, books, and content are specifically written for children, teenagers, or adults. Rarely do these resources provide content that will help you no matter what phase of life you are in.

Although finding resources specifically designed for one phase of life is helpful for certain questions, you might end up forgetting about what you have learned and never applying it to your life ever again. By finding resources that apply to your life both in the present and the future, you can begin creating the life you want, one day at a time, and constantly go back to the advice time and again.

Remember: Life is an act of creation, and it is your job to build it, no matter how young or old you are. The sooner you start grabbing ahold of life and creating the path you want, the more you will appreciate your life, what you have, and your decisions.

The purpose of this book is to provide you with a reference guide to everything you should know about life. This includes how to respect yourself and how to manage your relationships. The content you learn in this book can help make your life more impactful and meaningful so that you have the most successful boyhood and adult years possible.

To make reading this book a bit easier, I have separated it into four parts: Know Thyself, Health and Wellbeing, School and Work, and Relationships. From there, I break down the sections further so you can find our tips and tricks at a later date without much work. Each chapter is written with simple, easy-to-understand tips that will help you from the time you are a boy all the way until you have a boy of your own. With each chapter, I offer note sections and a question section to help you take what you are learning from this guide and apply it to your life directly.

While you are reading this book, I recommend talking to other boys and trustworthy adult figures in your life to get more tips and advice from those you trust most. Definitely consider asking your mom, dad, and grandparents. After all, they have a life full of advice that will help you out in the long run. Do not forget to talk to your friends about it too!

If you are a parent reading this for a child, I recommend initiating conversations with your son about some of the things you learned in this book. Although some advice might seem to go in one ear and out the other, your son will be able to pull out the information you tell them at a later date.

Without further ado, here are *101 THINGS EVERY BOY NEEDS TO KNOW*. I hope that this book can help you understand and navigate life with confidence and success.

Read the book from start to finish. Taking notes with handwriting in the margins will really help. Most e-readers allow you to write notes in the margin, which is very convenient. I recommend trying this out so you do not forget your own stories and advice you want to add.

CHAPTER ONE:

YOU ARE NORMAL

What You Will Learn: Even though you may feel weird, everyone is in the same boat as you, and you are normal.

One of the most difficult parts of growing up is getting to know yourself. Knowing the ins and outs of your personality takes time and experience. There will never be a time when you know yourself fully since you are constantly changing. Even so, you should strive to know yourself, no matter where you are in life. By knowing yourself, you can practice self-respect and live a life that you truly love and appreciate.

Part of getting to know yourself is accepting who you are as an individual and understanding that you are normal. While you are growing up, it is common to wonder if you are normal, question if those around you feel the same way, or feel like you are all on your own in terms of growing up and experiencing life. Although it is typical to feel these things, it is essential to understand that you are normal. Everything you have gone through and will go through is not entirely unique to you. Your family members and parents likely went through the same experiences back in the day, and your peers are going through the same thing now.

In fact, part of growing up is feeling like you are abnormal, despite the fact that you are completely normal. The faster you realize that you are normal, the faster you can begin creating the life you want and truly enjoying who you are. Here are five things to learn in order to understand that you are normal and apply this newfound information to your life.

1.

EVERYONE WONDERS IF THEY ARE NORMAL

The first lesson every boy should learn is that everyone wonders if they are normal. The very fact you are asking yourself this question shows that you are normal. Practically every individual through all cultures and times has felt the pressure of fitting in with their peers and growing up to be what is perceived as normal. Even the coolest guy at your school or the most successful individual in your office experiences times of doubt and wonders if they are normal.

So, accept the fact that everyone feels this way as soon as possible. When you accept that everyone wonders if they are normal, you begin to see people as they truly are, including yourself. You will stop putting people up on unnecessarily high pedestals and hold yourself to realistic standards. Needless to say, recognize that everyone around you wonders or has wondered if they are normal, and that is completely normal.

2.

"NORMAL" IS A MOVING TARGET

Even though everyone wonders if they are normal, there is no one set definition of normal. Normal is a moving target based on your age, friend group, and situation. As a result, there is no one way to be normal. Think about it this way: What is normal to you is not normal to your parents or someone the same age as you across the globe. Likewise, what is normal in one friend group is not always normal across all friend groups, even at the same school.

Understanding that there is no one set definition of normal can help you accept yourself and accept others around you. If something does not feel right to you, it probably is not right, even if it is the "normal" thing to do. Always remember that normal is a moving target so that you can be true to yourself in every situation.

More so, keep this fact in mind if you run across someone who you think is weird. For all you know, they may think you are weird too. Since normal is a moving target, try to keep an open mind and be kind to everyone you come in contact with, even someone who seems a bit odd or abnormal.

3.

FIND FRIENDS THAT MATCH YOUR NORMAL

Whenever you are making friends, remember that "normal " is a moving target. By keeping this in mind, you can find friends who you truly connect with, can be yourself with, and match your normal. When you find friends that match your normal, the friendships are easier, and you can enjoy your life. If friendship feels forced or you have to be someone else for the friendship to work, you have not found your group yet. That does not mean writing off the person, but it means you should keep looking for people who match your normal.

This advice is a lot easier said than done, though. If your definition of normal does not match the mainstream, you might have a bit more trouble finding friends that match your normal, and that is perfectly OK. You will just need to be more patient while trying to find your people. In the meantime, be open to other people and have an open mind. That way, you do not become lonely or bored while searching for your forever friends.

4.

MOST PEOPLE ARE TOO FOCUSED ON THEMSELVES TO WORRY ABOUT YOU

Whenever you mess up or do something strange, the first thing you probably think is, "I hope nobody saw that." Although this is a normal reaction when you do something embarrassing, you do not have much to worry about. Most likely, nobody noticed you, and if they did, they likely understand what you were going through. The truth of the matter is that most people are too focused on themselves to worry about you and what you are doing. Just as you are self-conscious, so are the people around you.

Once you truly take this information to heart, you can begin to be more forgiving and lenient towards yourself. Instead of caring about what other people think, only care about what you think. After all, they more than likely do not care anyway. Use this as momentum to live the life you want.

5.
FOCUS ON LIVING YOUR LIFE

Because most people are too focused on themselves to worry about you, you should spend your time and energy focusing on living the life you want to live. Do not focus on the life your parents want for you or the life your friends pressure you to have. Instead, your life is yours to live, and you get to make the decisions and steer the boat.

Do not get swept away worrying about what other people think of you either. Since most people are not thinking about you in the first place, do not waste any energy worrying about it. Focus all of your energy on living your life so that you can make the most of every moment ahead of you.

REVIEW

Whenever you are getting to know yourself, it is important to work through what normal means for you and how your definition of normal changes with time and situations. There is no need to put too much pressure on yourself when trying to learn who you are because everyone is in the same boat as you. Not to mention, the definition of normal is a moving target, and most people are too focused on themselves anyway. So, find people that match your normal and stay focused on your life, even when you feel a bit odd.

CHAPTER TWO:

DISCOVER YOUR VALUES

What You Will Learn: You must figure out your values in life since you have to live with the consequences of your actions.

Values are roughly defined as your set of principles or standards for behavior. Another way to define values is as your judgment about what is important in life. It is important for boys to understand what values mean and how they impact their lives. Although young boys may not be able to understand values completely, it is still important to for them to consider this concept. As boys get older, their values will change, and they will be able to have a better picture of what they value in life.

Even if you are not sure what your values are exactly, there are things you can do to begin learning where your values lie. There are also some factors you need to consider when determining your own personal values. Although caring about values may seem like a step far away, it is better to begin figuring out your values sooner rather than later.

If you wait until the time you are an adult to begin figuring out your values, it may already be too late. You might not have that strong of a character, or you may have already made serious mistakes that impact the rest of your life. By figuring out your values early, you can create the life you want.

All of that being said, values do change over time, and that is perfectly OK. The process of figuring out your values is an ongoing battle, and you should never become complacent. In other words, always continue to figure out your values and change them to fit your new approach to life and experiences. Through this effort, you can create the life you want and make decisions you are happy to live with, both now and in the future.

6.

ONLY YOU CAN DEFINE YOUR VALUES

The title of this chapter is "Figure Out Your Values." For a specific reason, we did not name this chapter "Figure Out Your Parents' Values" or "Figure Out Your Friends' Values." Instead, you have to define your own values since you have to live with your actions and their consequences. Only by defining your values will your actions follow your worldview, and you can live life in a way that makes sense.

Many people make the mistake of following values blindly. For example, many young boys will adopt the values of their parents without thinking about them. Although this sometimes works out, it often leads to less than ideal consequences. By the time that son is an adult, he may find himself confused, most likely because his actions do not line up with his true, personal value system. By defining your own values, you get to avoid this scenario now and as you grow.

That is not to say that you should not adopt the values of your parents at all. As we will discuss next, it is important to listen to the advice of those older and wiser than you. However, you should not just blindly adapt their values. Instead, you should look at the values, question them, and determine what they mean to you. That way, the values actually make sense to you and are applicable to your life.

If you do not get anything else from this chapter, get this: Only you can define your values, and you must define them if you want your actions and worldview to make sense.

7.
LISTEN TO ADVICE...

Even though it is up to you to define your values, it is important to listen to the advice of others. Your family members and friends have been in different situations and those older than you may be wiser. Their perspectives and opinions can provide insight that you would not have otherwise. It is imperative to ask for advice as a result. This advice can help you develop values on topics that you do not have any firsthand experience with.

For example, it is a great idea to ask your parents for advice if you find yourself in an ethical dilemma of sorts. You might also want to ask your teacher, friends, or other trusted individuals in your life. By asking a handful of people for their opinion, you get to listen to many stories, words of wisdom, and advice to develop an educated and thoughtful value criteria.

Although it may seem like overkill to ask for this much help, it can truly show you a more holistic picture of the issue. Consequently, your values will be more extensive and educated. Although it may be a bit embarrassing to ask for this advice, do not hesitate to do so.

8.

...BUT DO NOT BE AFRAID TO GO OFF ON YOUR OWN ROAD

Even though you should certainly listen to good advice, do not be afraid to go off on your own road either. Some advice you get will be fantastic and apply perfectly to the situation at hand. Other advice will be unrelated or outright bad. If you do not think the advice pertains to the situation or you do not feel that it is right, be prepared to go with your gut and go off on your own road.

Just because you decide not to take advice does not mean the discussion was a failure. On the contrary, the conversations you have with your family members and friends will be great memories that you cherish for a long time. You might even find out that the advice was great once you get a bit older. So, do not view the conversation as a failure if you decide to go off on your own road, but also do not take advice if something does not sit right with you.

9.

TRUST YOUR GUT

Knowing when you should follow a trusted family member's advice or go your own way can be a difficult task. Sometimes, the answer may seem obvious to you. Other times, you may have conflicting thoughts and feelings about the matter. Unfortunately, it never gets easier to determine what you should do when you are confused or unclear about a situation. When you find yourself in this situation, you should trust your gut. Nine times out of 10, your gut opinion is the right opinion.

If you are not sure what you should do in a given situation, try this: Do not think about the options, possibilities, and consequences. Instead, just say your gut instinct. If you cannot force your mind to be quiet, have a friend help you out. Have the friend pester you by saying something like, "Speak, do not think," until you are forced to answer. This answer is your gut instinct, and it is the advice you should follow if you feel conflicted on a matter and do not know whether or not you should follow someone else's advice.

Of course, certainly consider your gut instinct if you have the time. Asking yourself why you feel this way and running through possible consequences can further help you establish your values and land on the right choice of action in the given scenario.

10.
VALUES RELATE TO LIFE EXPERIENCES

There will be a time in your life when you talk to someone whose value system or worldview makes absolutely no sense. Everyone finds themselves in this scenario at one point or another. Instead of getting angry and trying to berate the other person about their values, remember that values relate to life experiences. What this means is that the values someone holds directly relate to that person's experience with life, situations, and relationships. In other words, there is a reason for their thought process.

By remembering this fact, you can be more understanding and open-minded when talking to other people who hold different values than you. It is important to note that being open-minded does not mean changing your values necessarily. Instead, it means treating the other person with the respect you would want in return.

Interestingly, remembering that values relate to life experiences can also help you uncover your values and hold them properly. As you are deciding on your values and thinking about issues, think about why you are landing on these principles and what situations in your life have contributed to them. Asking these sorts of questions can help you further understand yourself and improve your value system. At the same time, ask yourself what someone in another position would say. Would they agree or disagree with your value? This effort can help put your value into perspective.

REVIEW

Values are an important part of life. A man without values is like basketball without a ball: it does not mean much. Part of getting to know yourself involves determining what your values are and being able to live them out. However, this is easier said than done since establishing your value system is an ongoing process, and it is not always a black and white issue.

Even so, there are things you can do to help develop your value system as you grow. Most importantly, remember that only you can define your values. Although it is important to take advice from other people, do not be afraid to go your own way because you are the one who has to live with your actions. Just go with your gut and remember that values directly relate to your life experiences.

CHAPTER THREE:

THINGS CHANGE;
YOU CHANGE

What You Will Learn: Be prepared for change because it is an unavoidable part of life.

So far, I have talked about how you have to discover yourself and use your values as the basis of your life decisions. However, it is important to understand that your concept of self and values should constantly be changing. That is because as things change, you change. Because change is an unavoidable part of life, you have to know how to deal with change and what mindset to have about it.

If you are afraid of change and never want to let go, you will end up disappointed, stressed, and potentially unhappy with life. One way you can avoid this scenario is by recognizing that change is a part of life and embracing it with open arms. Once you recognize that change is unavoidable, you can learn to go with the flow and embrace everything life throws at you.

In this chapter, you are going to learn important facts about change, including how life changes, you change, and those around you change. You can use this information to constantly embrace yourself and improve your understanding of yourself as time marches on.

11.
CHANGE IS UNAVOIDABLE

Change is unavoidable in life. The faster you learn this fact, the better. Trying to create a constant life is absolutely impossible, and the effort will lead to a lot of dissatisfaction, regret, and pain. The only way to avoid this scenario is to recognize that change is a fact of life and that you have to learn how to embrace it.

Of course, you will not be able to predict all changes. Even so, have the mindset that change is going to happen, whether anticipated or not. That way, you are not caught off guard whenever change happens. It also means you will not be chasing an unrealistic expectation or standard in life.

12.
CHANGE IS HAPPENING
RIGHT NOW

To prove that change is unavoidable, I want to point out that change is happening right now as you are reading this book.

At this very moment, you are experiencing a change in your state. Every hour, humans shed about 600,000 particles of skin. In about seven years, you will have completely different skin cells from head to toe. Furthermore, your stomach lining sheds every three to four days. So, you will have an entirely new stomach lining in about half a week. Even your saliva is changing right now. Our bodies are constantly producing more saliva as we swallow and use old saliva.

These facts prove that change is an unavoidable part of life. It is literally ingrained in our bodies. To try to avoid change is an absolutely impossible task. Just as you do not fret over skin cells being shed, do not fret about other changes either. Instead, learn to expect change and not be too upset whenever it occurs.

13.

EXPECTATIONS MAKE FOR DISSATISFACTION

Speaking of expectations, it is easy to believe that dissatisfaction happens whenever things do not go your way. It is the world around you that is failing, not you. Although this view of the world is a common one, it leads to a lot of dissatisfaction and hurt. Not to mention, it is outright wrong. It is not the world that leads to dissatisfaction. On the contrary, it is normally your expectations of the world and life that lead to dissatisfaction.

Let us review the first sentence of this tip again to prove my point. "Growing up, it is easy to believe that dissatisfaction happens whenever things do not go your way." The operative phrase in this sentence is "whenever things do not go your way." This phrase implies some sort of expectation about what life should be and what you deserve out of it.

It is a simple fact of reality that life does not match expectations. Just because you have an expectation of life does not mean things will go according to plan. In fact, things are likely going to go a different way more often than they will go according to your plan. So, it is the expectations that breed dissatisfaction, not the world itself.

By being aware of this fact, you can begin to change your expectations of life. Instead of having unrealistic expectations about things out of your control, you can have hope that something will go one way, but you know that it might not. Whenever you provide an opportunity for things to go a different way, you are less likely to be disappointed.

How does this fact relate to change? Most people are not afraid of change itself. Instead, they are afraid of change that they did not account for. In other words, they are afraid of change that does not go according to plan or fit expectations. By changing your expectations, you can account for change so that you are not as afraid whenever it occurs.

14.

CHANGE IS A DOUBLE-EDGED SWORD

Change is a double-edged sword in the sense that it can be a positive thing or a negative thing.

On the one hand, change is often positive because it helps you grow and accomplish the goals you want in life. A good example of positive change is making a new friend or starting a new job. These changes are exciting and can help you be a better person. On the other hand, change can be negative because it is scary and sometimes hurts. Friends moving or a parent dying are examples of negative change.

People mainly only recognize negative change as true change. However, positive change is change too. Most people only fear negative change because it is the type of change that is not anticipated. Positive change, in contrast, is often welcomed with open arms. Although negative change certainly is not fun, it is important that you welcome it with open arms as well. After all, it is the negative change that sometimes helps us grow the most.

15.

YOUR OUTLOOK ON CHANGE MATTERS

Interestingly, your outlook on change largely determines which edge of the sword you get. If you are looking forward to a new job or want to make new friends, you will likely be excited when the positive change comes. This allows you to have a positive outlook on change in that situation. Most people do not think twice about their outlook on change whenever the change is positive.

It is a completely different battle when dealing with negative change. As we mentioned earlier, expectations breed dissatisfaction. In most cases, negative changes are associated with expectations. If you expect one thing but get another out of the change, you will likely view it as negative and wish that things went another way.

This fact further proves that you must manage expectations if you want to have a successful life. Only by managing your expectations will you be less disappointed whenever negative change comes your way. One expectation to specifically pay attention to in the context of this tip is your view of change as a whole. Instead of viewing some changes as negative and some as positive, look for the positive in everything.

Even though negative change is often painful and unwanted, it can do you a lot of good. It helps you grow, become a better person, and introduces new ways of looking at the world. These are all positive consequences of a negative change. By looking for the positive, you will not be as upset with the change, and you can begin dealing with your new life faster.

16.
IT IS OKAY TO FEEL SCARED OF CHANGE

Even though it is imperative to have a positive outlook on change, you will likely still feel scared of it in some cases. That is perfectly OK. In fact, it is normal to feel scared of change. There is no need to beat yourself up or feel weak just because change is a bit scary. If you were not afraid of change, that would be a lot weirder than being afraid of it.

Everyone loves what is known and comfortable. Change forces you into an unknown situation and often puts you in a state you are uncomfortable with. As a result, change is scary. The fact that change is scary is just about as unavoidable as change itself.

17.

CHANGE IS A PART
OF GROWING UP

Growing up is one of the most difficult parts of life. The main reason it is so difficult is that you are constantly undergoing change. Your body, mind, and your situation in life are changing. Change is practically at every corner of your life during childhood and your teenage years. To make matters worse, you have not quite learned how to deal with change yet.

That being said, change will continue to happen even in your adult years. Although the frequency of change is at its highest as a child, some of the most extreme changes happen in adulthood. In other words, change happens while you are growing up at every stage in your life. This can be what helps you grow up in the process. It teaches you new things and allows you to become the person you want to be.

Changes that occur when growing up certainly are scary. Once again, do not be ashamed of this fear, but recognize that this change is normal and is helping you to become the best version of yourself.

18.
ALLOW OTHER PEOPLE
THE CHANCE TO CHANGE

One of the most difficult parts of growing up is seeing those around you change and creating new relationships. As you get older, you will see your parents change before your eyes, feel relationships break apart, and see the impacts of other people changing. It is completely natural to resist this change and resent people as they change in their own lives.

Although this is a natural feeling, you have to allow other people the chance to change. Just as you are constantly changing, so are the people around you. To expect someone in your life to stay the same is impossible and harmful to both you and the other person. Allow other people the chance to change so that they can grow and become the best versions of themselves.

Just because you allow the other person to change does not mean you have to allow that person to stay in your life, though. If someone is changing for the worse, it is OK to separate yourself from that person so that you can continue changing for the better. However, you will find that some change in others is better, and you may drift towards new people as they change. I say all of this just to point out that your relationships with people are allowed to shift as they change.

19.

LET YOURSELF CHANGE

As you let other people change, let yourself change too. One difficult part of growing up is learning who you really are. From the time you are a child to the time you are in college, who you are will change dramatically. It is important to let yourself change so that you can become the best version of yourself.

After all, your body is physically changing at all times. As your physical body is changing, so too is your emotional, mental, and spiritual sense of self. Let your full being change along with your body.

While you are changing, your old friends may be resistant. If that is the case, it means that your friends have not learned the tip above. In that case, be true to yourself and allow yourself to change, even if those around you are pressuring you to stay the same. It is best to always allow yourself to change and grow as needed.

20.

LEARNING ABOUT YOURSELF
IS A LIFELONG JOURNEY

Because you are constantly changing, learning about yourself is a never-ending journey. Constantly try to learn more about yourself and adjust your values as needed. Even if your new values are completely opposite to what they were before, that is OK.

21.

FLEXIBILITY IS THE
KEY TO SUCCESS

Everything is changing, including yourself, those around you, and situations in your life. If that is the case, how can you succeed at your goals and become the person you want to be? The answer is rather simple: Be flexible in life because things change. Having too rigid of a sense of self and goals means you will end up failing whenever change comes.

To put it another way, be flexible with yourself, those around you, and your goals. Go with the punches whenever changes occur. If you need to come up with a new plan, then do so. It does not mean that you failed. It simply means that you took another course of action. By staying flexible, you will continue to progress even if changes completely devastate your past plans.

22.

EMBRACE EVERY MOMENT FOR WHAT IT IS

It is easy to feel overwhelmed and bogged down by change. In contrast, it is easier to live life without fear, regret, and stress whenever things are going your way. Unfortunately, change happens, and things may not go your way frequently. You have to learn how to embrace life, even when life is not matching your desires and expectations.

It is important that you learn how to embrace every moment for what it is. There is a time for change just as there is a time for stability. Embrace the change so you can make the most of it. Look at the change in a positive light, even if there is very little light visible. Embracing every moment for what it is will allow you to have a pleasing and satisfying life overall.

REVIEW

It is easy to get comfortable in your life and resist change. However, change is an unavoidable part of life. Even at this very moment, you are changing permanently. You must acknowledge the fact that change is always happening to yourself and those around you. Make sure your expectations with life are flexible enough to account for change. Only by learning to go with the flow will you have a satisfying life and grow to your fullest potential.

CHAPTER FOUR:

LEAD WITH RESPECT

What You Will Learn: You must develop self-respect so that you can lead and treat others with respect.

In today's culture, respect might not seem like that important of a characteristic. I am of the opinion that this is a travesty in our modern age. Respect is something that everyone must learn. You need to be able to apply respect to yourself. From there, you can then respect others.

Developing self-respect is an important part of growing up. It is how you learn to accept yourself and treat yourself as a person deserving of being treated right. If you do not respect yourself, you may find yourself in many scenarios that you are ashamed of or that hurt you. Once you learn how to respect yourself, then you will learn how to respect other people. Respecting other people is key to having healthy relationships.

In other words, respect is a vital part of a healthy life. You have to learn what respect is, how to respect yourself, and how to respect other people. If not, you may end up being tossed around like a plastic bag in the wind. Below, learn key facts about how to lead your life with respect.

23.

RESPECT IS A FORM
OF ACCEPTANCE

Respect can be a difficult concept to understand at first. In its very basic form, respect is a form of acceptance. Self-respect is when you accept yourself, whereas respect for someone else means that you accept that other person as a completely unique individual. If you ever hope to accept yourself as you are, you have to learn how to respect yourself. Furthermore, you have to respect yourself before you can respect someone else.

While you are getting to know yourself, it is important to have a healthy sense of self-respect. This means that you have to learn to accept yourself for who you are in your entirety. Wishing you were someone else or wishing you had different attributes is not showing self-respect. Instead, you need to respect yourself enough that you accept who you are.

Self-respect also applies to your sense of values and right and wrong. A person who has a lot of self-respect is not willing to compromise on their morals. Instead, they accept their sense of right and wrong and do what they know is right.

24.

DO NOT SACRIFICE
SELF-RESPECT FOR ANYTHING

Once you develop a sense of self-respect, do not sacrifice it for anyone else. As you are growing up, you will likely find yourself in scenarios where you are peer pressured to do something you feel is wrong. If you go against your values and give in to peer pressure, you are not respecting yourself. Instead, you are saying that your values are not worth being followed and accepted.

"What happens if I compromise my self-respect?" you may be asking. You will likely find yourself in situations you are ashamed of or embarrassed about. In the short run, you could get in trouble with your decision. In the long run, you could find yourself on an unhealthy path. In either case, you have to deal with the consequences of sacrificing your self-respect. So that you are happy with your consequences, do not sacrifice self-respect for anything.

25.

YOU HAVE TO RESPECT
YOURSELF BEFORE YOU CAN
RESPECT SOMEONE ELSE

When most people talk about respect, they discuss it in the context of respecting other people. Though it is imperative to respect other people, you cannot actually respect someone until you first respect yourself. Only by respecting yourself can you know what respect really is and apply it to other people.

Because of this fact, you need to begin cultivating a strong sense of self-respect from an early age. With self-respect, you will have a strong sense of right and wrong and acceptance, even in the light of unwanted scenarios. From there, you can apply respect to other people, even those you do not fully agree with.

26.

RESPECT IS THE KEY TO HEALTHY RELATIONSHIPS

Even though respecting other people begins with self-respect, you cannot forget about respecting those around you. Respect is the key to cultivating healthy relationships. You cannot have a healthy relationship if you do not respect the other party. Through respect, you can build feelings of safety, well-being, and friendship in your relationships.

It is important that you have feelings of respect towards everyone around you, including your parents, family members, friends, schoolmates, and acquaintances. At the bare minimum, you must be able to accept those around you for who they are, even if they are different from you. How you show this respect may differ from relationship to relationship, but respect should be the building block for all relationships.

27.
KNOW WHEN TO
WALK AWAY

Although you need to respect everyone around you, you do not need to sacrifice your self-respect in an attempt to respect others. You need to know when to walk away. You will most likely need to know when to walk away if someone lives in complete opposition to your sense of right and wrong and pressures you to do the same.

In this situation, still show the person respect. Allow them to make their own decisions and accept them for who they are. However, do not give in to their peer pressure, and do not make excuses for them. Instead, respect the individual for who they are, but do not forget about your self-respect along the way.

REVIEW

Respect is a vital part of knowing yourself and relating to those around you. Only by having a strong sense of self-respect will you be able to accept yourself and accept those around you. Even though you need to respect yourself and respect other people, do not sacrifice your self-respect for the sake of others. Know when to respectfully walk away, but keep respect as the building block of every relationship in your life.

CHAPTER FIVE:

ACCEPT AND UNDERSTAND YOUR BODY

As you are growing up, you will have to make terms with your body. It is difficult enough to accept your body as it is, but it can be even more difficult when your body is changing. During your preteen and teenage years, your body will undergo significant changes. You have to know how to handle your body and take care of it.

As I covered above, you have to accept yourself in order to respect yourself and respect those around you. Learning to make peace with your body is just one way that you can accept yourself as you are. Of course, this is easier said than done. It is normal to feel uncomfortable and awkward with your body, especially when it is changing. Although this is normal, it is important to push through these feelings so that you can accept your body as it is.

28.

YOU ONLY HAVE ONE BODY

As you grow and go through life changes, one thing will always be with you: your body. Throughout your entire life, you will only have one body. It is your job to take care of your body so that it stays as healthy as possible for as long as possible. It is important that you start caring for your body from a young age so that it is healthy and can last a long time.

On top of caring for the one body you have, you also need to appreciate it. Many people waste time hating their bodies and wishing they were different. Not only are these thoughts a waste of time, but they are unhelpful and do not show that you respect yourself. Think about everything your body does for you. It helps you run, play, sleep, and stay healthy. Thank your body for everything it does by appreciating it.

So, you have to learn how to appreciate your one body both from a physical and mental standpoint. Take care of your body so that it stays healthy, but appreciate your body so that you do not hate yourself in the process.

29.

YOUR BODY CHANGES

Being on good terms with your body is difficult because your body constantly changes. Once again, your cells are constantly being replenished. In fact, the body you have now will be made up of completely different cells within seven years. During your preteen and teenage years, your body undergoes some of the biggest changes.

It is important that you come to terms with your body throughout all of its changes. Although certain times may be awkward and uncomfortable, it is important to recognize that these changes are for the best. Even once you grow out of the teenage years, your body will still continue to change. Especially as you become a parent and grandparent, your body will change at rapid rates, and you might not even recognize the body you see yourself in.

Whenever this happens, call to your memory all the things that you learned from the changes chapter. Just as the world around you changes, so too does your body. Learn to love your body through all of the changes. As your body changes, you may even need to adjust how you care for it. Pay attention to your body and learn how it changes so that you can properly care for your body through all of life's twists and turns.

30.
YOUR WEIGHT IS
JUST A NUMBER

It can be easy to get bogged down by your weight and the number you see on the scale. Although you certainly want to be a healthy weight, do not get too fixated on the number itself. Instead, you want to focus more on fat content. The fat is what is dangerous, not the weight.

Not to mention, focusing on the number does not help you much. The reason for this is that muscle weighs more than fat. Some people may be incredibly slender and in shape, but they may weigh more than someone else who is in less physical shape. The reason for this is that they have more muscle mass, which leads to a higher weight overall. So, do not trust the number on the scale exclusively. You also need to consider your fat-to-muscle ratio.

The best thing to do if you are concerned about your weight is to talk to a doctor. A doctor will be able to explain if you are at a healthy weight or not. From there, focus on improving your health, not just the number on the scale. Fixating too much on the number often results in poor diet, eating disorders, and unhealthy relationships with yourself.

Even if the doctor tells you that you need to lose some weight, still love and appreciate yourself. You are more than you weigh. Certainly, get your weight under control through diet and exercise, but love yourself regardless and show yourself the respect you deserve.

31.

LEARN HOW TO TAKE CARE OF YOUR BODY

Since you only have one body, learn how to take care of it from an early age. If you wait to start taking care of your body until you are in middle age, a lot of damage will already be done. Your joints, skin, and even brain could already have irreversible damage that follows you through the rest of your life.

Instead of harming your body through food and actions, learn how to take care of it. There are many things you can do on a daily basis that nourish your body and keep it healthy and strong. How you eat, how frequently you sleep, and how you care for your mental health will all impact how your body functions today, tomorrow, and in the future.

Learning how to take care of your body changes with time. When you are a preteen and teenager, you will need more sleep than when you are an adult. You will also have to invest your time in more personal grooming. However, once you are an adult, you will have to pay more attention to your weight and medical health.

Although learning how to take care of your body may seem boring, it can actually be a lot of fun. Even if it is not fun, future, you will be thankful since your body was well taken care of in its youth. Plus, caring for your body is a great way to thank it for all the work it does, and it shows self-respect.

REVIEW

It is important to make peace with your body from an early age. In youth, it is easy to hate your body and wish you looked like someone else. However, you are only born with one body. It is important that you care for it properly through all of life's twists and changes. The earlier you begin caring for your body, the longer your body will work and function as it should.

CHAPTER SIX:

EAT RIGHT TO FEEL RIGHT

Once you come to terms with your body, you cannot just be complacent in your actions and self-care. Instead, you have to go the extra mile to actually care for your body and make sure it stays in peak condition. One of the best ways to care for your body is to eat correctly. What you eat directly impacts how you feel and how your body functions. By fueling your body with the right food, you will have the energy and health to accomplish all of your goals.

32.

YOU ARE WHAT YOU EAT

You have probably heard this saying before, but it is one that rings true. You are what you eat. The substances you fuel your body with directly impact how you feel, how you function, and how your body cares for itself. As a result, it is imperative to fuel your body with substances that are nourishing, healthy, and helpful.

To have the best diet possible, you want to have a well-balanced diet of vegetables, fruit, protein, fat, and carbohydrates. Any diet that outright prohibits a certain food group is likely unhealthy. According to the Harvard School of Public Health, about 1/2 of your plate should include vegetables and fruits, 1/4 of your plate should include whole grains, and 1/4 of your plate should include healthy proteins.

Some good foods to incorporate into your diet include:

- Broccoli
- Kale
- Green beans
- Sweet potatoes
- Apples
- Berries
- Bananas
- Whole wheat
- Barley
- Wheat berries
- Quinoa
- Oats
- Brown rice
- Fish
- Poultry
- Beans
- Nuts

It is OK to use some healthy plant oils in moderation as well, including peanut oils and olive oils. These oils can add a bit of flavor to your food, but do not go overboard with them.

33.

MOST DISEASES
ARE CAUSED BY DIET

To prove just how important it is to have a well-balanced diet, remember that many diseases today are actually caused by the Western diet. Heart disease, diabetes, and stroke are all examples of diseases primarily caused by diet.

Because so many diseases are caused by diet, you can keep yourself healthy just by ensuring you have a well-balanced diet. By following the healthy eating advice mentioned above, you will be able to minimize many diseases that plague our society.

34.

DO NOT DEPRIVE YOURSELF

For the most part, you want to always stick to eating a well-balanced diet that includes healthy portions of vegetables, fruits, whole grains, and healthy protein. You want to keep processed foods, sugar, and fatty foods to a minimum. Too many of these harmful foods are what can lead to the diseases mentioned above.

However, you do not want to deprive yourself of foods you love. Having too restrictive of a diet often causes people to give up and bounce back to even unhealthier eating habits than before. What this means is that you should have a diet that is primarily filled with healthy foods, but it is OK to treat yourself every now and then.

Let us say that you love pizza. Pizza, in general, is not a healthy food, but you do not have to ignore it completely. Once a month or so, it is completely fine to eat a slice of pizza. Just make sure to eat the pizza in moderation, and stick to a great, well-balanced diet the rest of the time. Eating a primarily healthy diet but treating yourself occasionally ensures you have a happy, healthy, and satisfying relationship with food.

35.

DO NOT FORGET ABOUT WATER

I cannot talk about the importance of eating right without mentioning water intake. Many people today are severely dehydrated because our culture as a whole does not drink enough water. As a rule of thumb, you want to drink between half an ounce and one ounce of water for every pound you weigh. So, drink between 50 and 100 ounces of water every day if you weigh 100 pounds.

If you really want to take your health to the next level, try to drink a glass of water before you go to bed, as soon as you wake up, and about 30 minutes before every meal. The water will ensure that your organs are functioning as they should, and it will prevent you from overeating.

Keep in mind that water consumption does not just include drinking pure water. Every time you drink tea, juice, or coffee, you are drinking water as well, but these drinks often include sugars and other ingredients. It is important to keep your sugary beverage intake to a minimum because it is easy to overindulge on sugar when it is in liquid form.

As for coffee and tea, be sure to drink these in moderation. Coffee and tea contain an ingredient called caffeine. Caffeine is perfectly healthy in moderation, but you can quickly become addicted to it if you drink too much. For most of your meals, try to drink water, but treat yourself whenever you are craving another drink.

The one drink type you should try to avoid entirely is soda. Soda is damaging to your teeth and organs, and it is addictive. Instead of drinking soda, opt for fresh juice, water, tea, and healthier drinks.

REVIEW

If you want to have a healthy life, you have to eat right. Make sure to have a well-balanced diet that is comprised mainly of vegetables, fruit, whole grains, and proteins. Do not forget to drink a lot of water and ignore soda. It is OK to treat yourself every once in a while but stick to your healthy diet on a day-to-day basis. If you follow these tips, you will be able to keep yourself healthy and prevent many diseases caused by diet.

CHAPTER SEVEN:

GET ACTIVE

You cannot just eat healthily and expect to have a healthy lifestyle. You also have to get your body moving and stay active. Staying active helps your muscles build and allows your body to be lean and flexible. There are a lot of ways to get active. It does not matter what you do, so long as your body is moving and grooving.

36.

BE ACTIVE EVERY DAY

To have a healthy lifestyle, it is important to be active every day. Only through daily, consistent activity will your body function as it should. It is important to get your blood pumping and lungs working every single day to keep your muscles healthy and fit. Sporadic activity will not help your body too much.

So, make it a goal to be active every day for about 30 minutes. If you are active for about 30 minutes every day, you will be able to maintain a healthy lifestyle. Make sure that these 30 minutes of activity include moderate to intense physical activity. If you go above 30 minutes, even better, but do not overdo it.

37.

GET OUTSIDE

One of the best ways to be active is to just go outside and have fun. In today's society, so many people are trapped indoors, staring at TV screens, computer screens, and other digital technology. Although this technology is a blessing, it is important not to forget about the blessings outside provided by nature.

Getting outside is important for your health and wellbeing. It helps to elevate vitamin D levels, reduce blood pressure, reduce inflammation, and improve sleep. Not to mention, it is a lot easier to be active and burn calories when you are outside. Needless to say, getting outside is a great way to improve your health and wellbeing.

Something as simple as going on a walk can allow you to get outside and be active every day. If you have a pet, ask your parents if you can take that pet for a walk. You might also want to consider riding your bike, jogging or even reading outside. Any opportunity you have to be outside, take it.

38.

FIND ACTIVITIES
YOU LOVE

If you do not love working out, that is OK. You do not have to be a gym fanatic in order to be healthy and live an active lifestyle. All you need to do is find activities that you love. There are tons of activities that can get you moving and active without feeling like work. I, personally, hate working out, but I love dancing, walking my dog, and swimming at a lake. All of these activities count as an active lifestyle, even though they do not feel like actually working out.

It is important that you find activities that you love that get you moving and feeling active. There are plenty of activities to choose from. Here is a list of different activities that are fun, do not feel like a workout, and get you active:

- Sports
- Walking
- Dancing
- Frisbee
- Hiking
- Exploring
- Rock climbing
- Water balloon fight
- Walking dog
- Jumping rope
- Yoga
- Hula hooping
- Cleaning
- Boxing
- Trampolining
- Swimming
- Paddle boarding
- Kayaking
- Bike riding
- Gardening

All of these activities are super fun, but they will also keep you moving. Try out new activities to find out which ones are your favorite, and make sure to do at least one every day for 30 minutes.

39.

FIND FRIENDS TO BE ACTIVE WITH

Making sure to be active and healthy can be difficult when you are doing it alone. You can make the process a little bit easier by finding friends to be active with. Your friends will make the activities seem more fun, and they can be a source of accountability on the days you do not want to exercise or be active at all.

Whenever you are young, it should be very easy to find friends to be active with. You can join sports teams or find other schoolmates that have similar interests as you. Join a team or a club so that you can get active with other people your age. Once you have a group of people you love to be active with; you will not feel like you are working out any longer.

As you get older, you may find it is a little bit more difficult to find friends you can be active with. However, you are not without options. Talk to coworkers who have similar interests. You can also join gyms that have group fitness classes. Even community rec centers often offer adult activities, such as gardening clubs and sports leagues.

40.

DO NOT PUSH YOUR
BODY TO THE LIMIT

We cannot overstate how important it is to have an active lifestyle. However, you do not need to push your body to its limit. It is important that your body always has the rest and recovery it needs. If you push your body to the limit, that is when injuries occur. Learn to read your body and rest when it needs to rest.

REVIEW

Part of having a healthy life is to get active. It is important to be active every day. Although this may sound daunting at first, it is a lot easier than it sounds if you get outside, find activities you love, and find friends to be active with. Just make sure not to push your body to its limit. Aim for about 30 minutes of moderate to intensive exercise every day to have a healthy and well-maintained lifestyle.

CHAPTER EIGHT:

YOU NEED SLEEP

Something that every young boy needs to know is that they need sleep. Children, preteens, and teenagers like to stay up late, have fun, and resist going to sleep. Although this may sound great at first, it is actually very damaging to your health and wellbeing. It is important that you have rejuvenated, restful sleep every night.

That being said, figuring out how much sleep you need can be a bit difficult. How much sleep you need will change based on your age, activities, and other variables. So, it is important to listen to your body. No matter what age or situation you find yourself in, it is still important to get enough sleep every night because lack of sleep takes a serious toll on your health.

Make sure to pair an adequate amount of sleep with a healthy diet and an active lifestyle to have a healthy body and life.

41.

LACK OF SLEEP TAKES A TOLL ON YOUR HEALTH

Sleep plays a vital role in our lives. It essentially functions as our body's recharge system. While you sleep, your body and mind can recharge so that you are refreshed and alert upon waking up. With a healthy sleep schedule, your body will remain healthy so that you can fight off diseases. Without enough sleep, your brain and body will not function properly, and you can experience short-term and long-term consequences as a result.

In the short term, a lack of sleep results in a lack of alertness and daytime sleepiness. Just missing an hour and a half of sleep at night will impact how you feel. Your memory and overall mental function will decrease the next day. You may even experience relationship stress due to moodiness, and your quality of life will decrease. These are just the short-term effects of lack of sleep.

If you continue not getting enough sleep, you can experience some serious side effects and problems. Some side effects of chronic sleep deprivation include high blood pressure, heart attack, diabetes, stroke, and even heart failure. Obesity, reduced immune function, and depression are all associated with sleep deprivation as well.

To make matters worse, not sleeping enough even impacts your appearance. Not getting enough sleep leads to wrinkles, dark circles under your eyes, and even acne.

In other words, failing to get enough sleep every night takes a serious toll on your health. In the short term, it will impact your quality of life, but it can lead to irreversible side effects if you continue to not get enough sleep.

42.

LISTEN TO YOUR BODY

Because sleep is such an essential part of our lives, it is important to listen to your body and provide the rest it needs. The good news is that your body does a great job of telling you when it is tired.

Some obvious signs that you are tired include feeling fatigued or sleepy. Feelings of stress, irritability, forgetfulness, and indecision are also signs of needing sleep. Your body will tell you it needs to sleep through physical symptoms as well. Tiredness, headache, sore muscles, dizziness, and slowed reflexes are all signs that you need to go to sleep.

If you feel tired or have any of the symptoms above, it is time to go to bed. Whenever your body tells you it is tired, listen. Once again, that is the only body you have. When it is tired and needs rest, give it the rest it needs to care for itself properly.

Once you start listening to your body, it will get into a groove, and you will know when it is time to go to bed. Once you get to that point, create a bedtime routine so that you can sleep easily and soundly. Turn off all digital devices an hour before bed, and try to have a 20-minute wind-down time. Some people like reading or writing before bed, whereas others like stretching. Experiment with different activities to find out which ones help your body get a restful night's sleep.

43.

HOW MUCH SLEEP
YOU NEED CHANGES

It can be difficult to determine how much sleep you need because the amount of sleep you need changes night to night, year to year, and phase to phase. Many different factors impact how much sleep you need, including your age, social life, obligations, genetics, and activity during the day.

As a rule of thumb, you should try to sleep between 7 and 10 hours every night. The exact amount of time you need to sleep ultimately depends on your age and activity levels. Here is a look at some general sleep guidelines according to age:

SLEEP GUIDELINES BY AGE

• **Birth to 3 months:** 14 to 17 hours

• **4 to 11 months:** 12 to 16 hours

• **1 to 2 years:** 11 to 14 hours

• **3 to 5 years:** 10 to 13 hours

• **6 to 12 years:** 9 to 12 hours

• **13 to 18 years:** 8 to 10 hours

• **18 to 64 years:** 7 to 9 hours

• **64 years and older:** 7 to 8 hours

Keep in mind that this is just a sleep guideline. One person who is 15 may need 10 hours of sleep, whereas another 15-year-old may only need 8 hours of sleep. Your genetic makeup and activity throughout the day will impact the exact amount of sleep you need.

Just listen to your body and learn your natural sleep schedule to get a better idea of how much sleep you need every night.

REVIEW

Even though it is important to be active, it is just as important to rest and sleep. Whenever we sleep, our mind and body recharges and rests. Without sleep, our quality of life and health may suffer drastically. As a result, listen to your body when it is tired and actually go to sleep. Make sure to adjust the amount of sleep you get based on your daily needs and changes in life.

CHAPTER NINE:

DO NOT FORGET ABOUT MENTAL HEALTH

When it comes to caring for your body, you cannot forget to care about your mind and brain too. Mental health is just as important as your physical health. Luckily, most people today talk about the importance of mental health, and there are tons of resources available for those who struggle with such issues.

Interestingly, one's journey with mental health begins from a young age. If you begin learning new techniques for caring for your mental health and stress, you will be better off as an adult. So, do not forget about your mental health whenever you are focusing on your physical health. The two go hand in hand, and your quality of life will largely increase when you begin focusing on improving your mental health.

44.

MENTAL HEALTH IS A SERIOUS MATTER

In the past, mental health was largely ignored and seen as a sign of weakness. Today, most people know that mental health is a serious issue that is just as important as physical health. In the United States alone, nearly one in five adults live with some sort of mental illness. For adolescents, one in seven experience mental disorders at some time. These statistics show just how common mental health issues are in today's society.

Furthermore, mental health has some devastating impacts on one's quality of life. You may not enjoy life and resort to harmful behavior as a way of coping with your mental health crisis. This behavior ends up affecting those around you as they see you struggling and want to help. Mental health can impact your physical health too. You may put yourself in danger, or your physical health may decline alongside your mental health.

I say all of this not to scare you. Instead, I tell you this, so you understand just how serious mental health is. You should put the same amount of care and attention into your mental health as you do your physical health. The consequences of failing mental health are just as serious as failing physical health.

45.

HOW YOU CARE FOR YOUR BODY IMPACTS YOUR MENTAL HEALTH

It is important to note that mental health and physical health often go hand in hand. How you care for your body, for example, impacts your mental health. If you never leave your room, never go outside, and only eat junk food, your mental health will likely suffer. That is because you are not helping your body produce the hormones and getting the activity it needs in order to stay healthy.

Conversely, how you care for your mental health is often reflected in your physical health. Obesity, eating disorders, and other similar physical health issues are all reflections of one's mental health. What this means is that it is important to care for your mental health and physical health together with equal importance. If you only pay attention to your mental health, you likely will not be caring for yourself entirely. Likewise, only caring for your physical health will neglect your mental health.

If you notice that your mental health is struggling, begin by paying attention to your physical health. Do you get enough exercise, water, and healthy food? If not, make sure to improve these areas of your life. Although improving your physical health will not fix or cure diagnosable mental illnesses, it will give your body the best shot at being healthy and healing your brain.

46.

CALM YOUR INNER VOICE

In addition to paying attention to your physical health, you need to learn how to calm your inner voice. Many mental health issues are caused by the way one talks to themselves. Do you have a negative inner voice that always tells you about your failings and shortcomings? If so, your inner critic will likely cause a lot of problems down the line if it has not already. Learn how to calm this inner voice so that you can talk to yourself positively and uplift your spirit.

At first, calming your inner voice will likely be very difficult. It often feels awkward and uncomfortable. Nevertheless, fight through this awkwardness and learn how to talk to yourself in an uplifting way. It is a good idea to ask yourself, would you say this to a friend? If you would not say something to a friend, you should not say it to yourself.

Overall, you want to have a kind inner voice that builds you up. Although you should not lie to yourself or ignore your shortcomings, there is no point in beating yourself up. Calm your inner voice so that you can learn how to talk to yourself in an uplifting and helpful manner.

47.

MANAGE STRESS

One of the most important parts of managing your mental health is learning how to manage stress. Stress is something that never goes away in life. From the time you are born to the time you are a wrinkly old man, there will be stress in your life. You must learn how to manage your stress to improve both your physical and mental health.

Stress alone is responsible for a number of diseases. In the short term, stress can lead to high blood pressure, headaches, and anxiety. In the long run, it can lead to heart problems, skin conditions, diabetes, asthma, depression, and arthritis. Because of how serious these side effects are, it is important to learn stress management techniques from a young age.

There are tons of different ways that you can manage stress. Not procrastinating and making the most of the time you have is a great way to manage stress because it ensures you do not have too much to do at one time. You should also be able to cope with stress through breathing techniques and activities like journaling. You can even use exercise and physical activities as a physical outlet to manage your stress.

It does not matter how you manage your stress as long as it is healthy, uplifting, and effective. Never manage stress through unhealthy means, such as overeating or substance abuse. Instead, opt for beneficial ways to manage your stress so you can live a healthy life and improve your mental health.

48.

DO NOT BE AFRAID TO ASK FOR HELP

Improving your physical health, calming your inner voice, and managing stress are all ways that you can improve your mental health. Unfortunately, these techniques do not work for everyone. It is important to know when it is time to ask for help, and do not be afraid to ask for help when you need it. This fact is really important for boys to understand since boys often feel that they have to be strong at all times.

The need for mental health help is not a sign of weakness. Just as you would ask your coach for batting advice, you should be able to ask mental health professionals for help and advice when necessary. If you feel that you need serious help, talk to a trusted adult in your life. A trusted adult will help you to get the medical care and attention you need to tackle your mental health problems head-on.

REVIEW

Caring for your mental health is just as important as caring for your physical health. The mental health crisis is at an all-time high, and it is important that you take it seriously. You can help improve your mental health by caring for your physical health, calming your inner voice, and managing your stress. Do not be afraid to ask for help when you need it, though.

CHAPTER TEN:

SELF-CARE IS NOT JUST FOR GIRLS

Self-care is not something that boys typically talk about or hear about. Even so, self-care is an important part of caring for your physical and mental wellbeing. Self-care is not just for girls. There are tons of ways that you can care for yourself while still feeling masculine and confident.

Through self-care, you can heal your physical, mental, and spiritual health. In fact, self-care is one of the best ways to heal yourself from the inside out or the outside in. Without proper self-care, you will not be able to take a holistic look at your health and wellbeing.

49.

SELF-CARE IS AN IMPORTANT PART OF CARING FOR YOURSELF

In order to have a healthy lifestyle, it is important to look at your whole being, including your physical, mental, and spiritual self. If you only focus on your physical health, you are neglecting important parts of yourself that may need improvement. That is where self-care comes into play. Self-care can help you improve your entire self, not just one part.

50.

SELF-CARE MEANS CARING FOR YOUR PHYSICAL, MENTAL, AND SPIRITUAL HEALTH

As mentioned above, self-care involves caring for your physical, mental, and spiritual health together. Instead of just focusing on one thing, it allows you to focus on your entire being for optimal health and improvement. Because self-care should be approached in this way, it is important to have self-care activities that approach all facets of your being.

Running, exercising, and skin care can all be examples of physical self-care, whereas alone time or participating in hobbies can count as mental self-care. Spiritual self-care can include reading a religious scripture, attending church, or even sitting in silence and appreciating your own thoughts.

No matter what your preferred self-care activities are, just make sure you are caring for your whole being, not just one part of yourself.

51.

DO NOT BE EMBARRASSED ABOUT SELF-CARE

Many boys and men are embarrassed to try self-care because it seems unfamiliar. The reason for this is that many examples of self-care appear feminine. Though there is nothing wrong with that, some boys do not want to participate in self-care in the form of massages, bath times, and skin routines. It is important to note that it is completely normal if you want to participate in these things. After all, massages, bath times, and skin routines help to improve both your physical and mental health.

If that is not your thing, there are tons of self-care techniques that are not feminine or associated with girls at all. For example, having some alone time to work on your hobbies is an example of self-care. Reading the Bible or any other religious text can be considered self-care, too, if you are religious. In other words, there are tons of examples of self-care that you have nothing to be embarrassed about. It is important to take a hands-on approach and forgo any embarrassment so you can fully care for yourself.

52.

CREATE A SELF-CARE ROUTINE

It is important that you create a self-care routine from a young age. Many people do this without ever realizing it, including men. If you are more conscious about your self-care routine, you can select activities that truly nourish your body and soul so you can live a healthy lifestyle.

It is a good idea to incorporate self-care activities into your morning and nighttime routines. How you begin the day sets the stage for your day, and how you prepare for bedtime can help you sleep and minimize stress. You might also want to have self-care activities sprinkled throughout the day so you have an overall satisfying and enjoyable life. Once again, just make sure you have self-care activities that involve your physical, mental, and spiritual health.

REVIEW

Self-care is not just for girls. On the contrary, boys and men also participate in self-care. Do not be embarrassed about it. Instead, recognize that self-care is an important part of caring for your physical, mental, and spiritual self. Create a self-care routine so that you can heal yourself from the inside out.

CHAPTER ELEVEN:

SCHOOL IS YOUR FIRST CAREER

Many students do not take school seriously. It is not until they start getting college rejection letters that they realize they should have tried harder in school. You can learn from these students' mistakes by viewing school as your first career from an early age. Even if you never apply to college, viewing school as your first career can dramatically impact your work ethic and job prospects in the future.

Although school might not be very fun, you need to take it seriously. Pay attention during school, and make sure to do your homework. If you treat school like your first career and take it seriously, you will likely succeed in most areas of your life, now and in the future.

53.

SCHOOL IS NOT JUST FOR NERDS

Sometimes when you are in school, there is a misconception that only "nerds" care about it. Meanwhile, the "cool" kids focus on looks, appearances, and sports. This is simply not the case. School is for everyone because it helps everyone succeed in life, get an education, and achieve the goals they want to reach. It is important that you focus on school as a result.

Just because you care about school does not mean you have to sacrifice sports and having a good time. You can still play sports and have interesting hobbies outside of school. You just need to focus on school during the school day and finish your homework after. That way, you can get good grades while still enjoying the things you love most.

54.

READ, READ, READ!

If you are reading this book, great job. That tells me that you love reading. Still, I want to point out that it is imperative to continue reading now and in the future. Reading is great for your health, intelligence, and relationships. In fact, many child psychologists recommend reading because of how great it is for personal development.

If you do not believe me, consider these facts that prove reading really does matter:

- Reading helps you build vocabulary
- Reading reduces stress by 68%
- Reading improves creativity
- Reading improves critical thinking
- Reading improves concentration
- Reading improves writing skills

These are just a few of the benefits that come with reading. Do yourself a favor and keep reading. You do not just have to read the stuff that you get assigned in school. Find genres of books that you love and never quit. Even comic books count as reading!

55.

LEARN KEY SKILLS
IN SCHOOL

If you have to sit through school, you might as well make the most of your time there. Instead of daydreaming and wasting your time, actually, try to learn key skills. Classes like English and math are vital for having a well-rounded education. They can also help you in any field you pursue later on as a career.

School is not just about learning academic facts, though. School helps you learn many other functional skills, such as time management, organization, and forming friendships. Do not forget to pay attention to these skills that are going to stay with you for the rest of your life. There are even some classes you can take that can help you build other life skills. For example, study skills, gym, and home education can all teach you how to create a healthy, well-balanced life that you love.

What I mean is that you should make the most of your time at school by learning. Most adults wish that they would have taken their time at school seriously so that they would be more educated. Do not make the same mistake!

56.

TEACHERS ARE NOT OUT TO GET YOU

Many students feel like their teachers are out to get them, and they do not listen or respect them as a result. As an educator myself, I can tell you with complete certainty that teachers are not out to get you. Most teachers go into the field because they have a love for learning and want to help young minds receive an education. In other words, teachers want to help you.

If you feel like a teacher is out to get you, you might want to reflect on yourself. Often, students feel like this when they are outright disobeying the teacher, and the teacher has to get on to them. If this is the case you find yourself in, begin listening to the teacher more or ask for clarification. Teachers will be able to see your efforts, and they will be happy to help you and reward your behavior.

More so, do not be afraid to ask teachers for help. Teachers love more than anything when their students ask for help and show interest in the topic at hand. If you go to your teacher and ask for help, they will help you. If you need additional resources, teachers will likely have some you can use as well. Do not be afraid to utilize your teachers because they are at your disposal for this very reason.

Most professors, bosses, and people in places of power want to see you succeed. Be open and honest. Ask for help when you need it, and that help will most often be given freely. You just have to ask for it!

57.

KNOW YOUR LIMITS

Even though it is imperative to try your best at school, you want to know your limits. By knowing your limits, I mean you need to know what you are capable of and how far you can go. Knowing your limits can help you avoid unrealistic expectations. It can also keep you from slacking off and growing complacent in your education and job.

Most importantly, you want to know your limits so that you do not overwork and harm yourself in the process. Everyone needs to sleep, and everyone needs to eat. If your schoolwork and job are preventing you from life necessities, you are passing your limit. Make sure to focus on your physical and mental well-being first.

At the same time, know when you are underperforming. Underperforming and not reaching your full potential is a form of disrespect to yourself. It is important to try your best and always try to reach your limit so that you are constantly improving and being the best version of yourself possible.

58.

DO NOT STRESS TOO MUCH ABOUT SCHOOL

Speaking of knowing your limits, make sure not to sacrifice your mental and physical health over school or work. Although it is normal to feel stressed before a big test, you should not feel constantly stressed due to unrealistic expectations. If you feel that you are sacrificing your health for school, it is time to take a step back and reevaluate your expectations.

You can talk to an adult for advice if you cannot tell whether you are over-stressed from school. Most adults will be able to help you figure out if you are worrying too much. They can also help you find coping mechanisms so that you can still try your best in school without sacrificing your health in the process.

59.

APPLY WHAT YOU LEARN IN SCHOOL TO WORK

Once you begin working, apply what you learn in school to work. This may include facts and information you were tested on, but it may also include the indirect things you learned in the process, such as hard work and resourcefulness. That way, your school experience is not something that was useless. Instead, it is something that directly relates to your everyday work and life experience.

REVIEW

Even though you may be tempted to slack off during school, make the most of your experiences. Treat school like your first career. School will teach you valuable information that you can apply in the future to your life and job. Make sure to read and ask your teachers for help when you need it. Although you want to focus a lot of your attention on work, do not sacrifice your mental and physical well-being for the sake of school. Your health should always come first.

CHAPTER TWELVE:

GET ORGANIZED

As an educator and professional student myself, I can tell you with certainty that organization is key to success in and out of the classroom. If you are not organized with your resources, space, and time, it's more difficult to succeed in life, school, or work. That is why it is important to get organized.

School provides the perfect opportunity to try out different organizational techniques. You can find out a structure that works for you. Then, apply it to different areas of your life for maximum success. If you can find an organizational structure and techniques that work for you, you will certainly be able to succeed in and out of the classroom.

60.

WORK SMARTER
NOT HARDER

Many people have heard the phrase work smarter, not harder, but they do not actually know how to work smarter. Getting organized is one of the top ways that you can work smarter while saving resources, energy, and mental capacity. Most experts agree that staying organized can help you save time, money, energy, brain power, and stress. As a result, you can work smarter, not harder, when you stay organized.

Think about it this way. How much energy do you exert when you cannot find a pencil or when you forget about a test? If you stayed organized, knew where all of your things were, and knew when your tests were planned, you could use that energy for other things instead. For example, you could use that energy to study and ace the test instead of panicking over it.

To work smarter, not harder, you really need to focus on your organizational capabilities. I would estimate that organization is about 95% of what goes into working smarter, not harder.

61.

A CLUTTERED ROOM IS A CLUTTERED MIND

Think about how distracting your school desk would be if you had toys, cell phones, and other items piled up in front of you. Would you be tempted to pay attention to what is around you, not the thing in front of you or your teacher? That is why a cluttered desk is a cluttered mind. You always want to keep your working space organized so that you can stay focused and work smarter, not harder.

Of course, it is important to find an organizational system that works for you. For some people, having too much organization is stressful and does not lead to enough creativity. If that sounds like you, it is OK to have a little bit of clutter and improvisation, but you do not want your desk to be so chaotic that you feel stressed whenever you sit down.

On the contrary, create a desk and working area that inspires you to sit down and focus. For some people, that may be a desk that is completely free of all things except a computer and a pencil. For other people, pictures of loved ones and artwork may be required. Find a working space that works for you and really maximizes your potential.

On another note, do not just view your literal desk as your only workspace. Your workplace should include your entire working area. Think about the lighting, color scheme, and organization on your computer. In other words, do not forget a single aspect when creating a perfect working atmosphere.

62.

ORGANIZATION APPLIES TO TIME MANAGEMENT

One of the hardest parts of organization is time management specifically. Time management involves planning out your day so that you can accomplish all of your tasks by their assigned deadline. As a child, time management is very difficult because it is hard to know how long it will take you to do things. As an adult, time management gets harder as you have more responsibilities on your plate. Needless to say, time management is hard for everyone.

Even though time management is difficult, there are ways that you can enhance your skills. For starters, make sure you know what your schedule is and when things are due. Make a calendar or agenda your best friend. I personally function best whenever I have a physical agenda that I write in with a pencil. I know other people that prefer to use the calendar on their phone. It does not matter which method you select as long as it works for you.

Once you have all of your due dates lined out, do not procrastinate. Procrastination is what leads to stress and poor decision-making at work and school. Instead of procrastinating, start working on things as soon as possible so that you have a lot of time to focus on the assignment at hand. Whenever emergencies spring up, you know you will have more than enough time to finish the assignment if you have not already.

To fight procrastination, create a workspace and work routine that you can depend on every day. By this, I mean have a set time that you work every day, no matter what, so that you are doing your assignments little by little. It might be a great idea to work right after school while you are still in the school mindset. I personally like doing things early in the morning because my mind is fresh, and it kickstarts my day on the right foot. Choose a time and place that is best for you.

Once you know when you want to work daily, do a little bit every day. It is a lot easier to sit at a desk for 15 minutes a day than 5 hours in one day. If you need to get a lot done in one sitting, use the Pomodoro technique. With this technique, you will work with the following timer:

- Work on a task for 25 minutes.
- Break for 5 minutes.
- Work on a task for 25 minutes.
- Break for 10 minutes.
- Work on a task for 25 minutes.

- Break for 20 minutes.

Note: you can adjust the times so that they work for you.

Do not be afraid to ask for an extension if you need it. In both school and work, some flexibility is required if you plan ahead. However, do not rely on this every time. Only reserve extensions for times when you find yourself in an emergency and really cannot get the assignment done on time. In that case, do not be afraid to ask for an extension. The worst they can tell you is no.

Use all of these techniques together to create an extensive time management plan. If you hear of another technique that sounds useful for you, try that too!

63.

CREATE A SYSTEM
AND USE IT

So, you need to work smarter, not harder, by cleaning out your space and improving your time management skills. It is important to note that you have to find a system that works for you. Just because a system works for me, your parents, or your friends does not mean that system will work for you. Only by finding a system that works for you will you be able to effectively organize your items and time.

It is OK to experiment with different organizational systems. Once you figure out what works, stick to it and use it. By sticking to the system, you create a sense of constancy that is a lot easier to manage. It also can reduce stress. Furthermore, using your system consistently means that you will be working smarter, not harder, because you always have a fall-back plan. You do not even have to think about it because it comes naturally.

REVIEW

If you really want to succeed in school and work, make sure you get organized. You need to organize everything related to the job at hand, including your items, workspace, and schedule. When you organize your work and school activities, you will be able to work smarter, not harder.

CHAPTER THIRTEEN:

DEVELOP A GROWTH MINDSET

Developing a growth mindset is arguably the most important thing you can learn in school. A growth mindset is what will allow you to learn from your mistakes and keep going, even when the going gets tough. If you do not remember anything else from this book, this is what I want you to remember: Develop a growth mindset.

What exactly is a growth mindset? A growth mindset views intelligence, talents, and abilities as learnable traits that can be improved upon through hard work and effort. A growth mindset is the opposite of a fixed mindset. A fixed mindset is one that tells you traits are stable and unchangeable; no matter what you do, you will not be able to improve upon your talents.

Experts have found that students with growth mindsets are typically those that achieve the best grades and succeed outside of the classroom. Conversely, those with a fixed mindset are those that give up. It is important that you develop a growth mindset from a young age so that you do not get discouraged by your mistakes but learn from them.

64.

MINDSETS FOLLOW
YOU EVERYWHERE

Before I dive into the specifics of the growth versus fixed mindset, I want you to know that your mindset will follow you everywhere. Even though I am discussing a growth mindset in the context of school and career, your mindset will also apply to your day-to-day life, relationships, and overall view of life.

If you want to increase the quality of your life dramatically, one of the best ways to do so is by focusing on your mindset. If you develop a healthy mindset, that mindset will be with you from the time you wake up to the time you go to bed. There is no way you can escape your mindset. As long as you are conscious, the way you perceive mistakes and challenges will be there, either as something to push you forward or something to hold you back.

Because mindsets follow you everywhere, you need to develop one that is healthy, helpful, and conducive to a successful life. You want to beat out harmful mindsets that assume you are a failure or incapable of amounting to anything. By focusing on a positive mindset, you will be able to attack all parts of life with confidence and excitement.

65.

FIXED MINDSETS
RARELY SUCCEED

As I have already mentioned, a fixed mindset tells you that you have no way of improving your skills. It also tells you that you make mistakes because you are a failure, and you cannot grow from those mistakes. Fixed mindsets are considered unhealthy, unhelpful, and downright dangerous. If you have a fixed mindset, you are more likely to fail.

In fact, many experts believe fixed mindsets lead to a number of negative consequences. It provokes a sense of dissatisfaction and disappointment in life and self. After all, your mindset is constantly projecting that you are not good enough. That makes you feel bad about yourself, even if it is untrue. Furthermore, a fixed mindset decreases self-awareness. You immediately assume you are the worst and incapable, even if you are very talented and capable.

Fixed mindsets have a major consequence on your school and career life as well. It often encourages mediocrity, and it cuts off opportunities. You feel content just scooting by, and you do not feel like you can achieve anything higher. You end up settling on jobs and opportunities that are mediocre, leading to lower satisfaction.

Fixed mindsets even impact your relationships. If you view yourself as a bad friend, you will likely attract other people like yourself. As a result, your relationships will be mediocre at best, and they will not bring a lot of long-term satisfaction.

All of this shows just how damaging fixed mindsets can be. It is important that you squash your fixed mindset so that you can replace it with something more helpful and healthy, namely a growth mindset.

66.
GROWTH MINDSETS ARE THE KEY TO SUCCESS

If you want to succeed in life, you need to develop a growth mindset. A growth mindset tells you that talents, skills, and traits are learnable and can be improved. With hard work, you can learn from your mistakes and end up as a better student, scholar, worker, friend, or son.

67.
INTELLIGENCE CAN BE DEVELOPED

When you have a growth mindset, you view your intelligence as something that can be developed. Many students struggle in school because they do not believe they are smart. Because of this belief, they stagnate and do not push themselves to be better. With a growth mindset, you will be able to evaluate your current intelligence and work hard to improve it.

Being able to develop your intelligence is obviously important for school, but it is important for other aspects of life as well. When you view intelligence as something that can be developed, you will be able to develop stronger relationships and learn new skills on the job. You will be able to succeed in many facets of life because you always view yourself as being able to learn and develop new skills.

68.

MISTAKES ARE
A GOOD THING

Something else you will learn whenever you develop a growth mindset is that mistakes are a good thing. I know I sound a bit crazy saying this, but it is the truth. Mistakes are rarely bad. On the contrary, they are wonderful because they give you an opportunity to learn, improve, and think creatively.

Next time you make a mistake, do not get upset or view yourself as incapable. Instead, go back to the mistake and try to figure out why it was wrong. If you cannot figure that information out on your own, ask your teacher or another trusted adult. From there, try to develop your intelligence so that you do not make the same mistake again. You have now learned something new!

69.
DEVELOP POSITIVE SELF-TALK

The third thing you will learn when developing a growth mindset is how to talk positively to yourself. As I have already discussed, the last thing you want is to talk negatively to yourself. An overly harsh self-critic is one that is harmful to your mental and physical wellbeing. Unfortunately, negative self-talk typically spirals out of control to the point that you cannot control it anymore.

With a growth mindset, you will be able to look at new situations from an objective point of view. You will then be able to approach the situation with confidence, knowing that you were able to learn new things and learn from your mistakes. Your inner voice will not be telling you what a failure you are. It will help you figure out how to learn from your mistakes so you can become a better you.

REVIEW

To succeed in school and your career, you need to develop a growth mindset. A growth mindset is one that learns from mistakes and does not view failure as the end of the story. By developing a growth mindset, you will be able to increase your intelligence, learn from mistakes, and cultivate positive self-talk. Through all of these improvements, you will open yourself up to more opportunities, become the best version of yourself possible, and help others in the process!

CHAPTER FOURTEEN:

HARD WORK MEANS MORE THAN TALENT

One of the most important parts of developing a growth mindset is understanding that hard work is more important than talent. That aspect is so important that I wanted to create an entire chapter dedicated to that topic. In almost all walks of life, hard work really is more important than talent. You can use this information to become the best version of yourself possible and feel capable of improving yourself.

Let us look at an example. Assume that you do not think you are very intelligent in school. By using what you learn in this chapter, you will be able to improve your intelligence so that you increase your grades and feel more confident on the next test day. This information applies to other abilities too. You can apply what you learn in this chapter to sports, relationships, school, and practically everything else.

70.

TALENT IS USELESS ALONE

The first thing you need to learn and truly understand is that talent alone is useless. A person can be incredibly talented but never amount to anything if they do not have the work ethic and drive to pursue and further their talents. Do you think LeBron James became the best basketball player simply because he is tall and talented? No. LeBron James works hard and shows up to every game ready to go.

The same applies to you. You may be a very talented and capable individual. That is great, but your talent will not get you anywhere unless you are willing to work. There will come a time when you will be out of your element and need to step up to the plate. Hard work is what will compensate for lack of experience or talent when the time comes.

Because talent is useless alone, focus on cultivating a good work ethic, even when you feel competent and capable. If you have a good work ethic when things are steady, you will already know what to do when you feel confused or out of your element in any way.

71.

HARD WORK BEATS TALENT EVERY TIME

If you compare a person who is naturally talented to a person who works hard, the person who works hard will win almost every time. Initially, the talented person may win, but the hard worker will beat them out over time. You can use this information to your advantage.

In the case that you are not very talented in a particular field, keep working hard. Eventually, you will be able to beat the individuals who are naturally talented but lazy. Conversely, do not forget to work, even if you are talented. The hard workers will beat you eventually, and you will not have any way of catching up since you do not know how to work hard.

72.

TALENTED PEOPLE FAIL WITHOUT HARD WORK

When most people think of geniuses, they think of individuals who are talented and do not have to work at anything. This is simply not the case. Individuals who are considered a genius or expert in their field typically spend 10,000 hours of practice before reaching this level. This fact proves that a lot of hard work has to be done if you really want to be an expert in your field, even if you are talented.

Let's take a look at Thomas Edison as an example. Thomas Edison has become one of the most prolific inventors in all of history. You might assume that he was a genius and that everything came naturally to him. When he was in school, Thomas Edison's teachers actually said that he was "too stupid to learn anything." By the time he was in the workforce, he was fired from two separate jobs for being nonproductive. Even as an inventor, Edison made as many as 1000 unsuccessful lightbulbs before inventing the successful lightbulb. How does Edison prove that talented people will fail without hard work?

If he did not have a good work ethic and determination, he would have quit long before the 1001 lightbulb was successful. As a result, Thomas Edison, a talented man, would have been unsuccessful if he did not have a good work ethic to keep him going through the inevitable failures.

If you are successful and naturally talented, you need to take Thomas Edison's story to heart. Although you might be naturally talented and capable, you will make mistakes. If you do not develop a good sense of work ethic, you may give up before reaching your ultimate success. On the flip side, you will end up successful if you keep passing through the mistakes and learn from them.

73.
MOST SUCCESSFUL PEOPLE ARE HARD WORKERS, FIRST AND FOREMOST

Thomas Edison is not the only talented individual who had to work really hard in order to be successful. In fact, the vast majority of successful people today are hard workers, first and foremost. Although they may be naturally talented too, it is their hard work that pays off.

Just like Thomas Edison, NBA legend Michael Jordan is also an incredibly hard worker. Jordan spent his off-seasons by taking hundreds of jump shots a day. Through this work, Michael Jordan was able to perfect his jump shots, making him one of the most famous basketball players in history.

There are countless other successful people that prove this fact. Starbucks CEO Howard Schultz works 13 hours a day, GE CEO Jeffrey Immelt worked 100-hour weeks for 24 years, and Venus and Serena Williams were hitting tennis balls as early as 6:00 AM from the time they were seven and eight years old.

If you want to become great at whatever your passion is, you need to start working too. Because school is your first career, dedicate a lot of your time into perfecting your schoolwork and intelligence. If you have another passion, dedicate a lot of hard work into developing that skill so you can be great and constantly improve.

74.

YOUR WORK ETHIC IN SCHOOL WILL FOLLOW YOU THROUGH LIFE

Many students do not feel the need to work hard in school because they do not think it will actually apply to the rest of their lives. This is especially true of students who know they do not want to go to college or have careers that require a college degree. Even if you know that college is not in your future, the work ethic you develop in school will follow you through the rest of your life. For this reason, it is imperative that you really focus on your capabilities and develop a work ethic while in school.

As I have already discussed, there are tons of things you will learn in school that you will apply to the rest of your life. Reading, writing, and basic math, for example, are things you directly learn in school that apply to different facets of your life. You will also learn indirect things at school that impact your life, hard work being one of them.

If you do not think you will go to college, it is likely because you do not find school interesting, or it is simply not where your natural talents lie. If that sounds like you, you likely know from experience just how hard it is to wake up in the morning and care about topics you know you will not use directly in your future. However, it is important to fight through these feelings so you can develop a good work ethic.

If you can work hard on topics that you do not enjoy or see any use in, imagine how much easier it will be to work hard on topics that you love and excite you. School is the perfect opportunity to develop a great work ethic, even in the face of scenarios that bore you. Conversely, you might not know how to work hard if you slacked off all through school. Imagine being 18 years old and suddenly being asked to work hard when you never had to before. Fat chance you will learn than either!

In either case, the work ethic you develop in school will follow you through the rest of your life. So, it is important to develop this from a young age. Whether you go off to college, go to trade school, or choose another path in life, your sense of hard work and determination will follow you everywhere you go and allow you to succeed.

75.

EMPLOYERS CARE MORE ABOUT HARD WORK THAN TALENT

In today's job force, finding great workers is difficult. You can often find people who are really talented, but these talented people might not work hard or put in much effort. Conversely, hard workers may take a lot longer to perform tasks and lose productivity in the process. Most employers view the best employees as those who do the top work and are hard workers. In other words, you cannot just be one or the other.

If you are more of a hard worker than a talented person, you might think that this is a bad thing, but the opposite is true. Once you begin developing your talents through hard work, you will actually have talents that appear natural to someone who just met you. Thus, you will appear naturally talented. You will also have the ability to work hard since you have already developed that skill within yourself. In other words, hard workers appear to be both talented and hardworking because the hard work creates talent.

What this means for you is that developing a good work ethic in school can follow you through to your first job. Employers will be happy to work with you because you seem talented and eager to work. Coworkers will also like you because they know they will not have to pick up your slack. Most importantly, you will be excited to go to work because you know you are capable and competent.

REVIEW

If you really want to succeed in school, your career, and life, you need to develop a good work ethic. From basically every perspective, being a hard worker is better than being naturally talented. After all, a talented person with no work ethic means nothing. As Thomas Edison, Lebron James, and Michael Jordan all show, you have to be willing to put in the time in order to be great. Talent alone is not enough. By developing a great work ethic in school, you will be a hard worker in all facets of your life.

CHAPTER FIFTEEN:

PARENTS

As a boy, it is important that you know how to form healthy, respectful, and helpful relationships with your parents. Even if you do not live with your birth parents directly, you can still find parental figures in your life that can help you navigate these difficult waters.

Regardless of who your mom and dad are, it is important to have a good relationship with them. Your parents set the foundation for how you interact with other people. Learning how to understand your parents and interact with them can help you succeed not only as a son but in other relationships.

76.

PARENTS ARE STILL LEARNING TOO

As an adult, it took me a long time to realize that my dad is just like me. He is a human who is still learning and capable of making mistakes. As a child, I viewed my dad as someone who could do no wrong. Whenever he messed up, I felt that the mistake was a fault against me. This could not be further from the truth.

As adults, we will do our best to help you using the experience we have from our own lives. Your parents are still learning too.

They may not be perfect, but they are doing their best to raise you in an environment so you can be a confident, happy, and healthy young man.

77.

CUT YOUR PARENTS SOME SLACK

Because your parents are still learning, try to cut them some slack. I know it is tempting to throw a temper tantrum whenever they mess up, but they likely are beating themselves up over it more than you are. Most parents stay awake at night thinking about the things they could have done differently during the day.

The last thing your parent needs is for you to berate them about all the things they have done wrong. Trust me. They know far better than you about what they have done wrong. Instead of yelling at your parents, be a bit more understanding. They are doing their best to raise you while they are raising themselves in the process.

78.

TAKE THE TIME TO KNOW YOUR PARENTS

When I was in middle school, my mother died, and I never got the opportunity to know her. That is something that I have always felt sad about as an adult. I never got to know my mom as an individual. Because of this regret, I have done everything in my power to get to know my dad as an individual. I highly recommend that every young boy take the time to truly get to know their parents.

Getting to know your parents is an insightful and rewarding process. Parents can teach and guide you, but they can also be your friend. You will likely find that one of your parents, if not both, are incredibly similar to you and have many of the same life experiences. Even if you are different from your parents, the memories you share with them and the stories they tell you will last your entire life.

I definitely recommend sitting down with your parents as often as possible. Begin by asking about their childhood and getting to know them as people. As you get older, your bond with your parents will grow, and you will get to learn even more. Do what I did not get to do, and get to know your parents, both of them, as individual people.

79.

YOUR BIRTH PARENTS ARE NOT ALWAYS YOUR MOM AND DAD, AND THAT IS OKAY

Even though this chapter is about parents, I want to point out that birth parents are not always your mom and dad. That is perfectly OK. Whether you are raised by your grandparents, foster parents, or adoptive parents, everything that I have said so far applies to them as well. All that matters is that your parents love you and that they are doing everything in their power to give you the life you deserve.

I can say from experience that you do not need a close relationship with your birth parents to live a happy and satisfying life. So, do not be too upset if you do not have a close relationship with your biological parents if they are not available to you.

80.

GET ADVICE FROM YOUR PARENTS

When I was younger, the last thing I wanted to do was ask my dad for advice. I felt that he was too old and out of touch with reality to actually offer me any advice that worked. As I have gotten older, I have come to realize that this is far from being true. I wish I had gotten more advice from my dad growing up. I probably would have been better off if I had.

Learn from my mistake and get advice from your parents whenever you need it. That is exactly what your parents are there for, and they will be happy to help you when things get tough. All you have to do is ask, and most parents will be more than happy to help.

I know this will be a little bit awkward, but it is worth it. Your parent will appreciate the thought, and they will not judge you. If you do not have a parent to ask for advice from, talk to another trusted adult instead. Any trusted adult will be happy to help you out and provide you with the advice you need.

REVIEW

The first relationships you form with other people are the relationships with your parents. As a result, it is imperative to start building a strong relationship with your parents from the time you are young. Although you may be tempted to view your parents as the best version of humanity, they are just people too. Cut your parents some slack, and take the time to know them, even if they are not your birth parents.

CHAPTER SIXTEEN:

SIBLINGS

Your relationship with your siblings is also important. Second to getting to know your parents, your relationships with your siblings are arguably the most important relationships in your life. From experience, I can tell you that a great relationship with your siblings will last from the time you are young to the time you are old. Cultivating a great relationship with your brothers and sisters can help you have a sidekick through all stages of life.

If you do not have siblings, you are not without options. Cousins and close family friends can be transformed into siblings too. You just have to find people that will be with you from the beginning and be happy to be your sidekick through it all.

81.

YOUR SIBLINGS ARE
YOUR SIDEKICKS

If you are lucky enough to have siblings, try to treat them with the due respect they deserve so you can be lifelong friends. In fact, nobody will know what you have grown up with as intimately as your siblings. Because siblings grow up in the same environment, your brothers and sisters can become your sidekicks.

You should use this fact to your advantage. Instead of viewing your siblings as competition, join forces with them. Although this will certainly cause your parents a bit of a headache when you are younger, it is something that you will appreciate and cherish as you grow older.

82.

WORK TOGETHER

Because your siblings are your sidekicks, definitely work together. Two heads are always better than one. In some cases, three heads are better than two. No matter how many siblings you have, work together so that you can create lifelong bonds and have a lot of fun in the process. No matter how many siblings you have, try to include everyone.

83.

DO ACTIVE THINGS
WITH YOUR SIBLINGS

One of the best ways to bond with siblings is to get active with them. Go outside and make actual memories. Do not just sit inside staring at a computer or TV screen.

My best memories with my siblings involved getting outside and exploring the world around us. Whether you live in the country or in the city, find things you enjoy outside that are fun and exciting. Chances are, you all will be able to form memories that you will be laughing about until the time you are adults. Even my dad and his brothers still laugh about the mischief they got into while outside together, and I hope my sisters, my brother, and I will be the same way.

84.

ASK OLDER SIBLINGS
FOR ADVICE

If you happen to be a younger sibling, do not hesitate to ask your older siblings for advice. As an older sibling myself, I never looked down on my siblings for asking me questions. On the contrary, I looked forward to helping them. Your sibling will likely be able to give you some great advice because they were already in your footsteps.

85.

PROTECT YOUNGER SIBLINGS

If you are an older sibling, be sure to keep a close eye on your younger siblings. As an older sibling, it is your responsibility to help your parents protect your younger brothers and sisters. As they get older, they will appreciate the advice and help you provided them.

At the same time, do not be too much of a parent figure. Nobody likes being lectured by anyone who's not a parent. So, only act if you know your sibling is in trouble and needs help but also allow your sibling to make their own mistakes and live their own life.

REVIEW

Siblings are the real sidekicks in the world. Your siblings are with you through thick and thin, and they grow up in the same scenario as you. As a result, work with your siblings and get active outside. You will be able to create memories that last a lifetime. Do not forget to be good to one another. Younger siblings should go to older siblings for advice, and older siblings should be on the lookout for the younger siblings.

CHAPTER SEVENTEEN:

GRANDPARENTS

Whenever you are growing up, it is tempting to overlook your grandparents and feel that they are a burden. I know when I was growing up, I hated having to talk on the phone with my grandparents and spend the night at their home alone. I just felt that they were old, awkward, and no fun. Unfortunately, far too many grandsons feel this way about their grandparents.

As you get older, you will find that you have to cherish the time you have with your grandparents. Because your grandparents are so much older than you, you do not have a lot of time with them, but they have a lifetime of knowledge and fun stories for you to hear. It is important to form a great relationship with your grandparents so that you can have these memories as you grow older.

86.

GRANDPARENTS
ARE A BLESSING

Many people do not have grandparents anymore. As time goes on, grandparents pass away, and a lot of family history, knowledge, and stories are lost in the process. If your grandparents are still alive, view them as a blessing, and do everything you can to form a relationship with them and have one-on-one time.

If you do not currently have a relationship with your grandparents, it might seem a bit awkward at first, but it will certainly be worth it. Especially as you get older, you will learn to intimately appreciate the time you spend with your grandparents when they are still in good health. In the case that you already have a good relationship with your grandparents, do not take this for granted because many people cannot say the same.

If you do not have any living grandparents, that does not mean you cannot have a grandson-grandparent relationship with anyone. If you have great aunts, great uncles, or close family friends that are of your grandparents' age, you can have a relationship with them as well. I recommend following all of these tips, even if you do not have living grandparents, with someone that you can have a grandson relationship with.

87.

ASK ABOUT YOUR FAMILY HISTORY

One of the most important reasons why you should bond with your grandparents is that they have a wealth of knowledge about you and your family history that your parents might not even know. As people get older, they tend to care more about family lineages and histories, which is why grandparents specifically tend to know a lot about the family's past. Although this information might not interest you now, you will certainly want to know it later.

Once your grandparents pass on, that information will be lost forever. While your grandparents are still available to you, ask about your family history, their past, and their experiences so that you can get a full understanding of where your family came from and where it is going.

If more than one of your grandparents are alive, try to ask all of them about your family history. Each grandparent will have their own unique stories and memories to share. This can provide you with a lot of closure and intimate memories with all of your grandparents, not just one.

88.

FIND A WAY TO BOND WITH YOUR GRANDPARENTS THROUGH SHARED ACTIVITIES

In addition to asking about family history, try to bond with your grandparents through shared activities. At first, you might not think that your grandparents have anything in common with you. Upon closer inspection, you will find that there are many activities that you and your grandparents both enjoy.

For example, many granddads enjoy golf, baseball, and other sports. If you are a sports person, try to play with your grandparents or at least watch a ball game with them. Grandmothers tend to enjoy crafts, pictures, and family histories. Try to participate in some of these activities so that you and your grandparents can have a shared bond.

Even if your grandparents live far away, the joys of technology mean that you can bond with your grandparents from anywhere in the world. At first, your grandparents may be resistant to using technology, but they will likely be excited to learn it if it means they can spend more time with you.

REVIEW

Because of technology, you have no excuse when it comes to bonding with your grandparents. Do everything in your power to get to know your grandparents, learn about your family history, and form close relationships through shared activities. Doing these things with your grandparents will create memories that you cherish for the rest of your life.

CHAPTER EIGHTEEN:

FRIENDS

According to *Time* magazine, friendships are actually more important in life satisfaction than romantic relationships for most men. This tells us that having a few great friends is imperative for having a happy, healthy, and satisfying life, especially for boys. This makes sense given the fact that friends are one of the first relationships we learn about from a young age.

Even though friendship is such an important part of satisfaction in life, navigating friendships can be a bit difficult. Especially when you are surrounded by peer pressure and people who you do not really know, the task of finding friends that you trust and bond with can seem daunting. So, you can never overemphasize the importance of having valuable friendships, from boyhood to manhood.

89.

A FEW CLOSE FRIENDS ARE BETTER THAN MANY ACQUAINTANCES

When you are in school, it often appears that the cool kids always have dozens and dozens of friends. Following in line, many students strive to have as many friends as possible, even if the friendships are not very respectful or valuable. In these cases, you are not really dealing with friends. Instead, you are dealing with acquaintances.

For long-term satisfaction, having a few close friends is way better than having a lot of acquaintances. Though few in number, your close friends will be there when you need them, and you will actually be able to enjoy their presence and respect them properly. When you have a lot of acquaintances, you might be able to have a fun time with them, but you will not know if you can trust them, and you will not know them very well.

For these reasons, you want to focus on cultivating a few close relationships. These friendships are the ones who you can depend on when things get tough. They are also the friendships that will stand the test of time and be in your life for the long haul. Acquaintances, in comparison, are there for a good time but not a long time. They are good to have during your school day, but you need close friends you can text at night when you are upset.

90.

INTROVERTS NEED
FRIENDS TOO

As an introvert myself, I grew up thinking that I did not need friends in the way that extroverts do. By the time I graduated high school, I did not really have any friends. I had one or two acquaintances, but there was no one I could really depend on when I needed it. I thought that this was just a natural part of being an introvert. As I have gotten older, I realized that this was an unhealthy way of looking at things.

Just like extroverts, introverts need friends too. The only difference is that we only need one or two friends at a time, whereas extroverts enjoy being in social gatherings. The key to finding great friends as an introvert is to find other introverts too, though you can certainly be great friends with extraverts as well. When being friends with an introvert, that other person will understand that you do not like socializing too much or becoming overwhelmed.

91.
YOU ARE WHO YOUR FRIENDS ARE

Whenever you are selecting friends, it is important to choose your friends wisely. As the old saying goes, you are who your friends are. If you are constantly hanging out with mean, irresponsible people, you are likely going to turn out the same. Conversely, hanging out with hardworking, kind people will encourage you to be kind and hardworking as well.

Because you are so influenced by the people around you, select friends that you truly respect, admire, and want to spend your time with. Selecting friends in this way will help you be the best version of yourself. Likewise, you will help them to be the best version of themselves.

I will be the first one to admit that this is not a way to be cool or super popular. Being more selective about your friends means that you will ultimately have a smaller selection pool. Though you will have fewer selections to choose from, your friends will be much higher in quality.

You should still show everyone respect, even those that you do not think are a good influence on you. Once again, respect is the building block of all relationships. Just be aware if a person has too much influence over you or is being a bad influence. From there, be able to walk away respectfully so that you can maintain the values you hold dear.

92.

FRIENDS COME AND GO

It seems that the word I keep coming back to is change. This word applies to the concept of friendships as well. Friendships come and go and change with time. Although it is sad to see friends move and leave, we have to be open to change and be willing to see friends change as a result. This is simply an unavoidable part of life.

In fact, studies have found that the vast majority of childhood friendships do not last beyond high school. The reason for this is that everybody changes. As both people grow apart, there may not be enough similarities to keep the relationship going. Although there can still be great memories between the two of you, the relationships will change permanently.

This phenomenon is one that you might not experience until after you graduate high school or college. Once everyone begins going their separate ways, friends change permanently, and you will have to seek out new friends with people who have more in common with your current self and life.

REVIEW

The key to having a healthy, satisfying life is having fantastic friends. Unfortunately, navigating friendships can be a bit difficult. Everyone needs friends, but it is important to remember that having a few close friends is better than having a lot of acquaintances. The friends that are close to you are those that you will be able to depend on, day or night. Keep in mind that the friends you held close in the past may not be the same friends you have today, and that is OK. Time affects everything, including friendship.

CHAPTER NINETEEN:

COMMUNITY

When most people talk about relationships, they mainly imagine relationships with individuals. However, you can have a relationship with your greater community at large. In fact, having a positive relationship with your community can allow you to be a great individual and community leader.

Many people do not begin thinking about community involvement until they have to volunteer or are older in age and looking for friends. Focusing on your community involvement and relationship from a young age is a great way to foster community spirit and understand those around you. I always recommend young boys to get involved with their community so that they can be the best citizens and people possible.

93.

GET INVOLVED WITH YOUR COMMUNITY

When you are young, it is easy to focus on your friends, school, sports league, and those directly around you. Although these people and relationships certainly are important, do not forget to get involved with your community. Your community is just as important in bringing you up as those you have intimate relationships with.

There are many ways that you can get involved with your community. You can go to local sporting events, attend community festivals, or even volunteer at local organizations in your area. The options are limitless when it comes to getting involved with your community. Just find a topic you enjoy, and get involved. The process is actually a lot easier than you may think.

If you are a bit nervous about getting involved with your community, bring along some friends too. Getting friends and family members involved is a great way to lessen the awkwardness since you have someone there that you already know. Plus, it will help the community even more because you are bringing another community member into the fold.

94.

LOOK BEYOND THOSE DIRECTLY AROUND YOU

When I say "community," I mean everyone, even those you do not see or speak to. When most people think of their community, they think directly of their neighborhood, school, or church. These areas are part of your community, but there are many parts of the community you likely do not see.

For example, elderly patients at a nursing home are part of your community, and so too are the homeless people on the street. Although it may be uncomfortable to look beyond those you see, it is important to look for those who need help in your community. Even if you live in a safe, affluent community, there are people in your area that you may be overlooking.

Once you start looking for people beyond those around you, you will see just how much help your community needs to grow and prosper. Volunteer at organizations and get involved in local political matters. Even if you are not old enough to vote, you can still be a part of the change by educating those around you and just being a good citizen in general.

95.

COMMUNITY IMPROVEMENT BEGINS WITH YOU

Once you start looking beyond the community directly around you, you will see that a lot needs to be done. I am not going to lie; it is very stressful and overwhelming when you see how much there is to do. Even so, it is important to take matters into your own hands and be the change you want to see. To put it another way: community involvement begins with you.

Whenever you see the problems around you, it might be easy to point out the faults in everyone else. However, change begins with you. If you are not willing to change anything in your life, why should you assume that anyone else will? So, be the change you want to see and start impacting your community one action and person at a time.

As a child, you might not feel like you can do a lot, but that is not the case. You can be the change you want to see by volunteering and getting involved. Just talking about issues can do a lot of good. If you get involved, your family may get involved too, furthering the issue. Continue volunteering and getting involved as you get older. The older you get, the more you will be able to do.

Once you can get involved in politics, dive in. Most people focus all of their political energy on the federal level, but it is local politics that impact you the most. Focus your attention on the local level, and you will see a lot more change impact your daily life and the community at large.

All that I am describing actually has a name. It is called active citizenship. Active citizenship is when people get involved with their local community at all levels. Active citizenship can be something as small as cleaning up your street or educating young people about democratic values. What matters is that you are getting involved directly and trying to be the change you see. Strive to be an active citizen to improve your community on all levels.

REVIEW

The last relationship to focus on in your life is your relationship with your community. Although it might sound weird thinking of having a relationship with your community, it is an important part of being a boy and growing up to be a great man. Get involved with your community, but look beyond those you see directly. Once you get involved, be the change you want to see in your community to transform your future.

CHAPTER TWENTY:

PRACTICAL SKILLS

At the end of the day, there are skills that you should know to help you get through a tough situation or possibly even a tough day. Learning and practicing practical skills is important to everyone, even if you don't think that you are going to end up stranded in the woods one day. These next few skills will aid you on your next camping trip, in case of an emergency, or even in times when your power goes out.

96.

HOW TO FISH

Even if you don't like eating fish, knowing how to fish is useful if you ever find yourself in a situation where it is the only food source you have. Fish provide a lot of good nutrients and will fill you up in times of need.

When fishing, there are a few key tools that you will need: a fishing rod, lure, bait, and a container for the caught fish. Choose a fishing rod that is sturdy and can handle a lot of pulling. While a cheap rod might be easy to get, you don't want there to be a chance of your fishing rod snapping in the middle of reeling in a fish. Also, choose a lure that matches the water you will be fishing in. In preparation, have several different colors of lures so you can choose once you get to the water. You can also use bait instead of a lure.

If your rod comes with a bobber, great. If not, go and get one because the bobber will tell you that you got a fish. Once you get the line into the water, you will know that you got a bite when your bobber starts moving up and down. Use the reel on your rod to pull the line in, making sure that you can feel the tug of the fish through the whole process. Reel your fish up and out of the water, putting it into your container if you are keeping the fish to cook.

97.

HOW TO CLEAN FISH

Always clean your fish before cooking. Unclean fish can have tons of bacteria, and most people don't want to eat fish scales.

The first step to cleaning fish is to thoroughly wash the oil and grime from the outside of the fish's body. Pat it dry with paper towels before setting it onto the cutting board. Many people recommend taking a knife and slicing away the scales. Using a butter knife and long, fluid motions is the quickest way to descale. After this step, rinse off your fish again.

Your fish is ready for whatever you decide next. Whether you cook your fish as a steak or filet, it will require different preparation methods.

98.

HOW TO PACK
FOR CAMPING

Following a list is essential for packing to go camping; otherwise, your risk of forgetting something is super high. When you pack for camping, make a list of everything that you think you'll need. As you add stuff to your supplies, you can check that item off. If you are at a loss for what to bring, there are many online checklists that you can print off and use. Make sure to triple-check your list and your supplies.

Make sure to remember a light source, tools (you never know what will happen,) a water filter, several layers of clothes, a first aid kit, dental hygiene products, sunscreen, and personal identification. Of course, there are so many other things to bring, but some of the above items should not be forgotten.

99.

HOW TO USE A COMPASS

Compasses are amazing tools to give you direction and prevent you from getting lost. Have your map and a compass with you whenever you go traveling through the wilderness. Always break your directions into smaller steps to better find where you need to go.

First, place your compass onto your map so that the baseplate matches where you want to go. Then rotate the dial until that north matches with the north on the map. This lines up the compass, so it gives you proper directions based on the map. Now, you can pick up the compass, have the red arrow match the orienting arrow, and follow that straight ahead. You will want to reorientate yourself frequently to make sure you are still going in the right direction.

100.

HOW TO TIE HELPFUL KNOTS

Knowing how to tie knots will help you whether you are camping or simply need to hold things together. Different types of knots are good to know, and we will go through each.

TYING A CLINCH KNOT

1. Pass the working end through the hook eye

2. Wrap it 5 times around the standing line

3. Pass it through the first loop

4. Pull it and the standing line to tighten

5. Cut off excess tag end

6. The knot it complete

Clinch knot: This is for attaching your hook to a fishing line. Loop the line through the loop of a hook, then with the line, loop it around the straight line 5 to 7 times. Bring the lines back to the bottom, where a loop will form and bring the line through. Tighten it, and you will have a tight knot.

PALOMAR KNOT INSTRUCTIONS

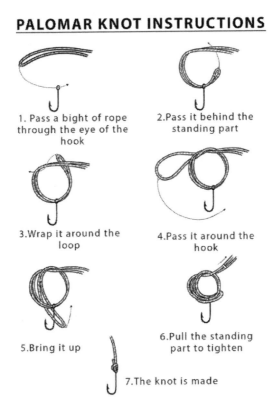

1. Pass a bight of rope through the eye of the hook

2.Pass it behind the standing part

3.Wrap it around the loop

4.Pass it around the hook

5.Bring it up

6.Pull the standing part to tighten

7.The knot is made

Palomar knot: Fold your fishing line in half and feed it through the loop of a hook. Fold the line that doesn't make a loop up and wrap it around the loop, then bring the loop down and through the hook. After that, tighten.

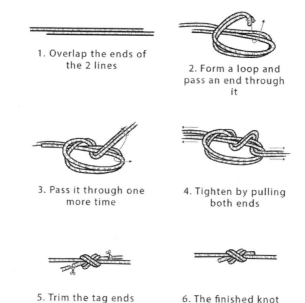

1. Overlap the ends of the 2 lines

2. Form a loop and pass an end through it

3. Pass it through one more time

4. Tighten by pulling both ends

5. Trim the tag ends

6. The finished knot is compact

Surgeon knot: Take two ends of your string and form a loop and pass the ends through the loop twice. Tighten the knot by pulling from both ends. This knot is similar to creating a pretzel.

101.

HOW TO BUILD A FIRE

Whether you are freezing cold or want to make dinner, knowing how to make a fire is essential.

First, you'll want to create a fire bed. This is a safe area that will keep your fire contained. A clear area with a circle of rocks makes a good fire bed. Then, grab good firewood. Look for sticks and small, dry logs. Dry grass and leaves make good tinder that will catch fire quickly.

Set up your fire by placing the tinder in the middle (all the dry and small stuff), then lay your sturdy logs in a pyramid shape around the tinder. This is one of the most common and easiest ways to set up your fire. Light up the tinder with a match or lighter (if using a lighter, light up a twig and throw it into the middle to keep your hands safe). Now you have a fire!

Recap

Practical skills are good for everyone to learn because they are... practical! Even if you aren't a nature or camping fan, you might end up in a situation where you will need to learn these skills. It's always good to learn how to tie a sturdy knot as that can help you with everyday things like loading up a truck bed with boxes. In the end, practical skills boil down to being organized and resourceful. Knowing what is available and what to do with those supplies can help you in any situation that you may encounter.

CONCLUSION

Growing up from the time you are a boy to the time you are a man takes a lot of effort, time, and decision making. There are many different relationships you need to focus on and skills you need to develop within yourself so that you can be the best version of yourself. This book can help you get one step closer to becoming the man you want to be.

REVIEW

The journey to becoming the man you want to be begins with knowing yourself. Remember that you are normal and that you need to figure out your own values. From there, develop a good sense of self-respect and treat others with respect in exchange.

Once you figure out who you are, focus on your health and wellbeing. This includes the physical, mental, and spiritual being. Make sure to eat right, be active, and get enough sleep. Do not forget about self-care.

You also have to focus on school and work. Your school is your first career. Even if you are not passionate about school, you can learn a lot about life, including how to get organized, how to develop a growth mindset, and how to be a hard worker.

The last thing we learned is about relationships. It is important to have a good relationship with your parents, siblings, grandparents, friends, significant others, and community. Although these relationships can be difficult to navigate, they will result in a healthier life that leads to a lot of satisfaction and happiness

FINAL THOUGHTS

I will tell you in advance that this takes a lot of work, time, and effort. Reading this book and even writing it is a lot easier than the journey of becoming the man you want to be. The process is ongoing and ever-changing. Even once you think you have hit the point you are satisfied with, you will continue to change, grow, and improve.

So, take this book and keep it with you. It might help you now, but it will continue to help you in the future. The journey will be long and hard, but it will be worth the fight by the time you become the person you want to be.

Made in the USA
Las Vegas, NV
23 December 2022

73R00074